Copyright (c) 2021

Title: The Monster on the wrong side of the bed
Written & Illustrated by Corina Giles

1st Edition, Print
ISBN: 978-1-957073-01-9

Published by PlayTime! A Therapy Center
products@richplaytherapy.com

DEDICATED TO
ALL SMALLS AND
FORMER SMALLS
WHO HAVE BATTLED THE
MONSTER ON THE WRONG
SIDE OF THE BED.

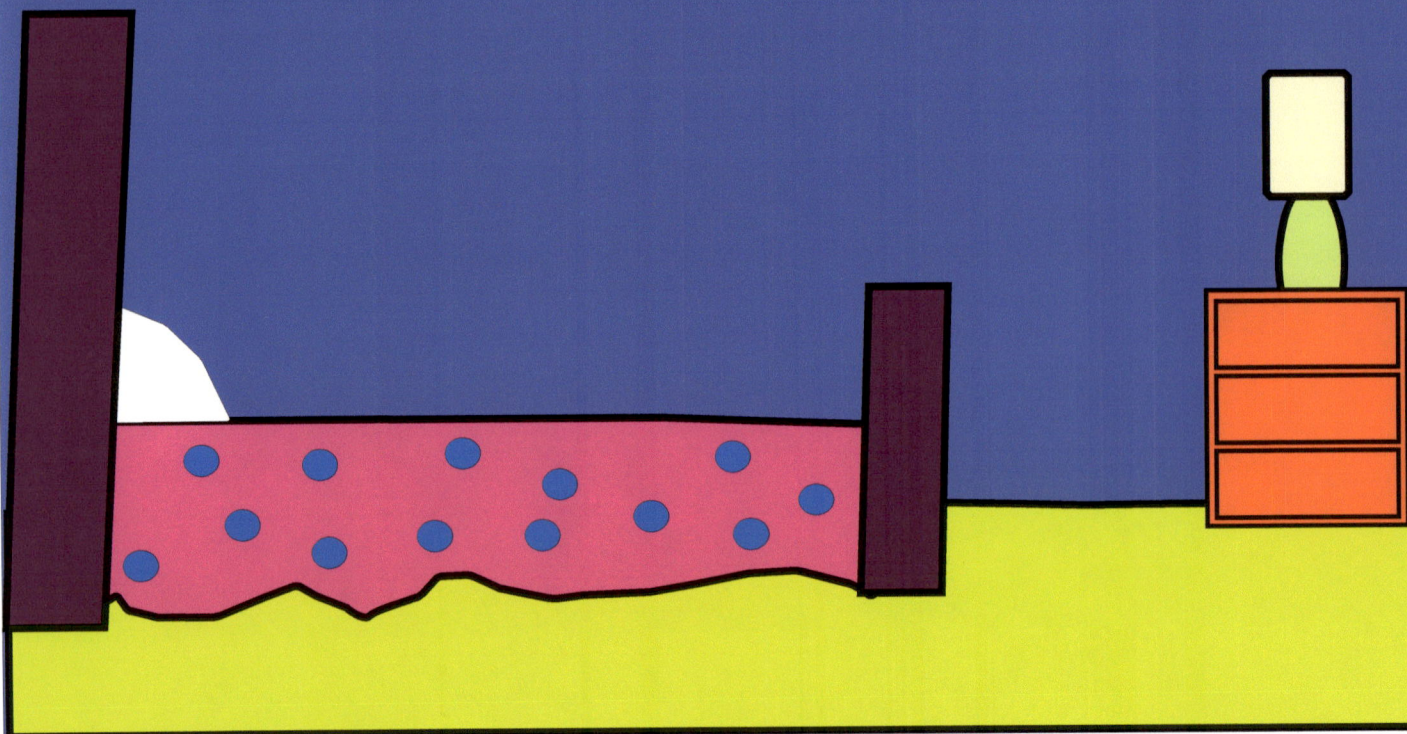

The Monster on the Wrong Side of the Bed

Written & Illustrated by
Corina Giles Ed.S, LPC, RPT-S

Playtime! A Therapy Center

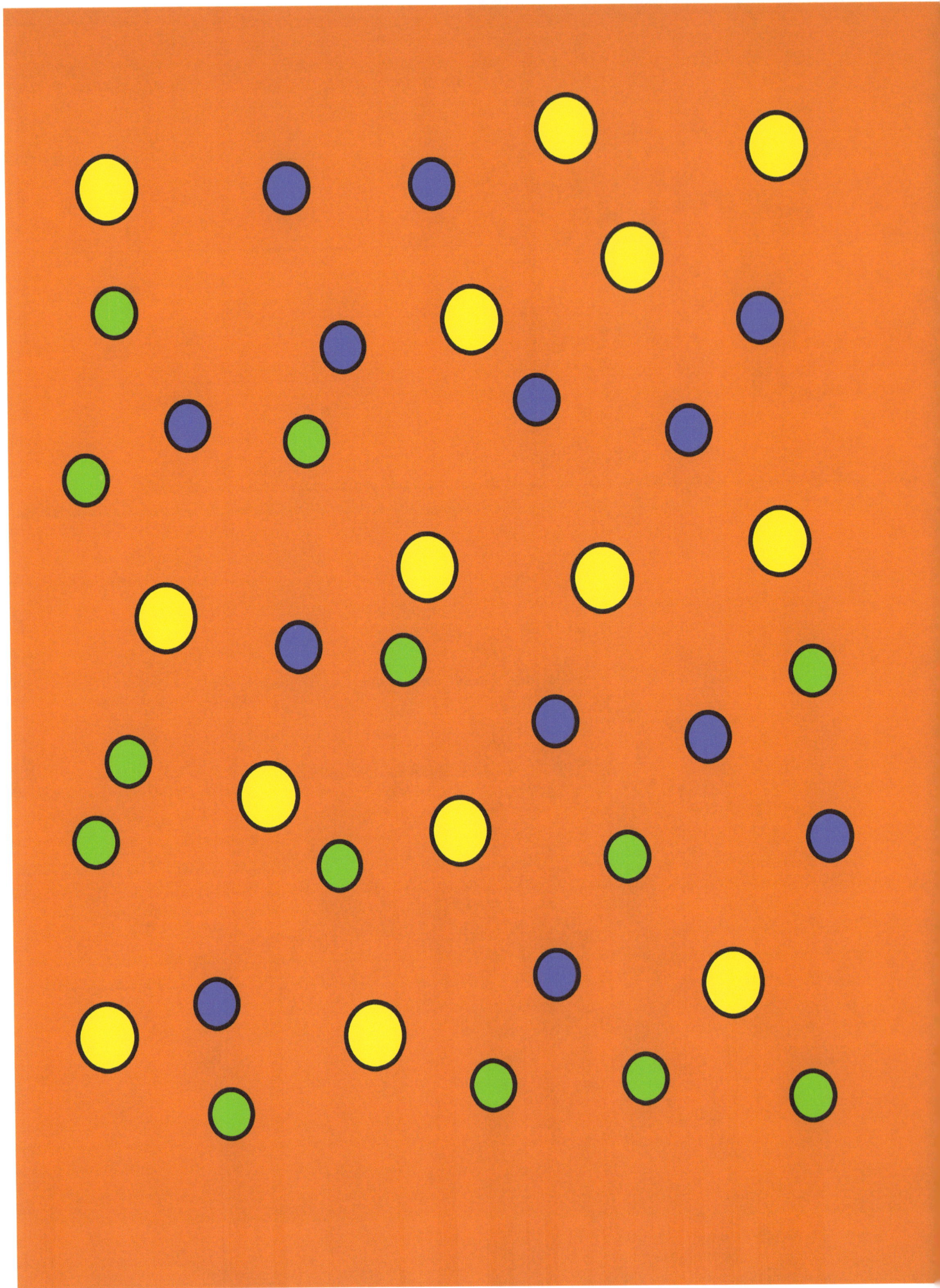

Sometimes we feel more than one feeling at a time. That is called crashing feelings.

This book is full of feeling words which have CRASHED TOGETHER to form new feelings.

Can you figure out which feelings have crashed together throughout this book?

Check your answers on PAGE 28 when you reach the end.

I'm grumpy this morning- beware!
The smile on my face- not there.

Last night I felt great,
but stayed up way too late.

I'm "SLUMPY"- no niceness to spare.

The bus is especially loud.
My best friend nowhere in the crowd.

I leave my pride on the shelf
and I sit by myself.

"LANXIETY" in me forms a cloud.

I daydream of climbing a tree.
No, no! Please don't call on me!

I drew trees on my work.
They all laugh- I'm biserk!

I'm "EMBRACTED" and just want to flee!

That kid Devin thinks he's so cool,
but I think he smells like old drool.

I wish he would leave—
his presence is such a pet peeve!

I'm "JEALEAN" and I want a new school!

On the playground I still feel upset
then a tap on my shoulder I get.

When I turn, I yell "HEY!"
then Devin asks me to play.

I'm "SORRAMED" and I'm filled with regret.

When I open up my lunchsack,
an extra treat my mom did pack.

Tension? There's none,
so with Devin I share one.

I feel "FRENEROUS" with his pat on my back.

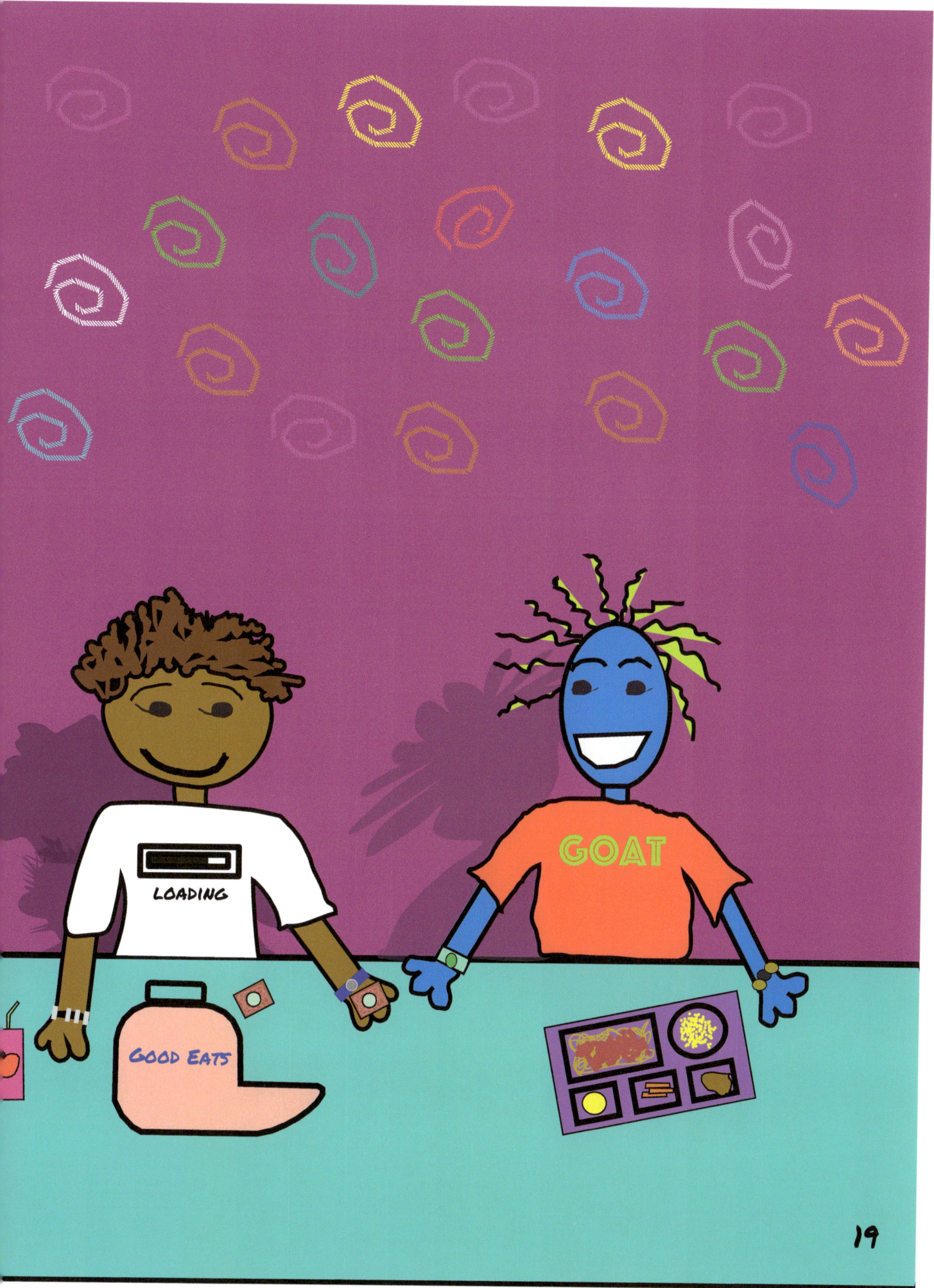

In P.E. she smiled and asked "Hey,
can I partner with you today?"

I said, "Cool", with a gleam.
We had fun- a great team!

I'm "COOLAPPY"- harsh feelings away.

That distraction- my brain ignores.
My focus- the teacher adores.

I start to feel proud.
No self-doubt allowed.

I am "SMOUD"- my confidence soars.

"So how was your day?" they all ask.
I say "It was a difficult task.

It started out hard-
all day I was on guard...

but "HOPALM" once I lost that monster mask."

Waking on the wrong side of the bed
can make bad thoughts fill your head...

but to save your day
push that monster away

and recharge your feelings instead.

HOW MANY "CRASHED FEELINGS" WERE YOU ABLE TO FIND?

SLUMPY= SLEEPY + GRUMPY

LANXIETY= LONELY + ANXIETY

EMBRACTED= EMBARRASSED + DISTRACTED

JEALEAN= JEALOUS + MEAN

SORRAMED= SORRY + ASHAMED

FRENEROUS= FRIENDLY + GENEROUS

COOLAPPY= COOL + HAPPY

SMOUD= SMART + PROUD

HOPALM= HOPEFUL + CALM

TALKING POINTS

After reading the story, take some time to discuss the following talking points with your child. Instead of verbalizing responses, encourage your child to draw or act them out.

1. How did the main character feel at the beginning of the day? How do you know he felt that way?

2. What was the first thing that happened to make the main character feel bad?

3. What could the main character have done to have a better bus ride after his friend wasn't there?

4. What are some things the main character can do to stay focused in class in school tomorrow?

5. What was really making the main character angry when he saw Devin?

6. At the end of the story the main character felt proud. What made you feel proud today?

7. Who was the monster on the wrong side of the bed? What made the monster go away?

www.ingramcontent.com/pod-product-compliance
Lightning Source LLC
Chambersburg PA
CBHW042130040426

42450CB00003B/146